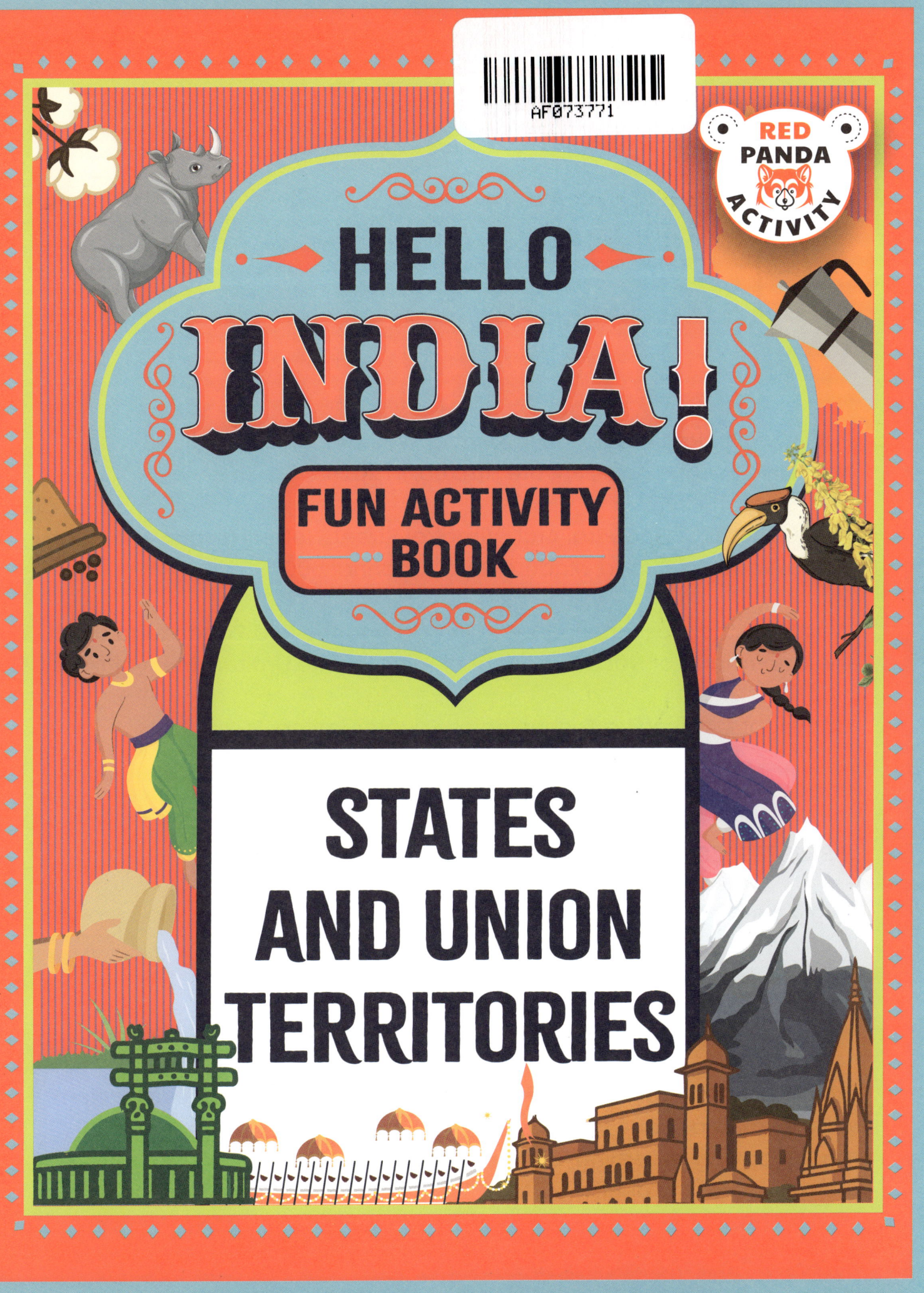

Published by Red Panda, an imprint of Westland Books, a division of Nasadiya Technologies Private Limited, in 2025

No. 269/2B, First Floor, 'Irai Arul', Vimalraj Street, Nethaji Nagar, Alapakkam Main Road, Maduravoyal, Chennai 600095

Westland, the Westland logo, Red Panda and the Red Panda logo are the trademarks of Nasadiya Technologies Private Limited, or its affiliates.

Copyright © Nasadiya Technologies Private Limited, 2025

Images sourced from Shutterstock

ISBN: 9789360452711

10 9 8 7 6 5 4 3 2 1

All rights reserved

Printed at Nutech Print Services, India

No part of this book may be reproduced, or stored in a retrieval system, or transmitted in any form or by any means, electronic, mechanical, photocopying, recording, or otherwise, without express written permission of the publisher.

WHERE'S MY CAPITAL?

Know your states! Match the highlighted states to their capitals and place them on the map.

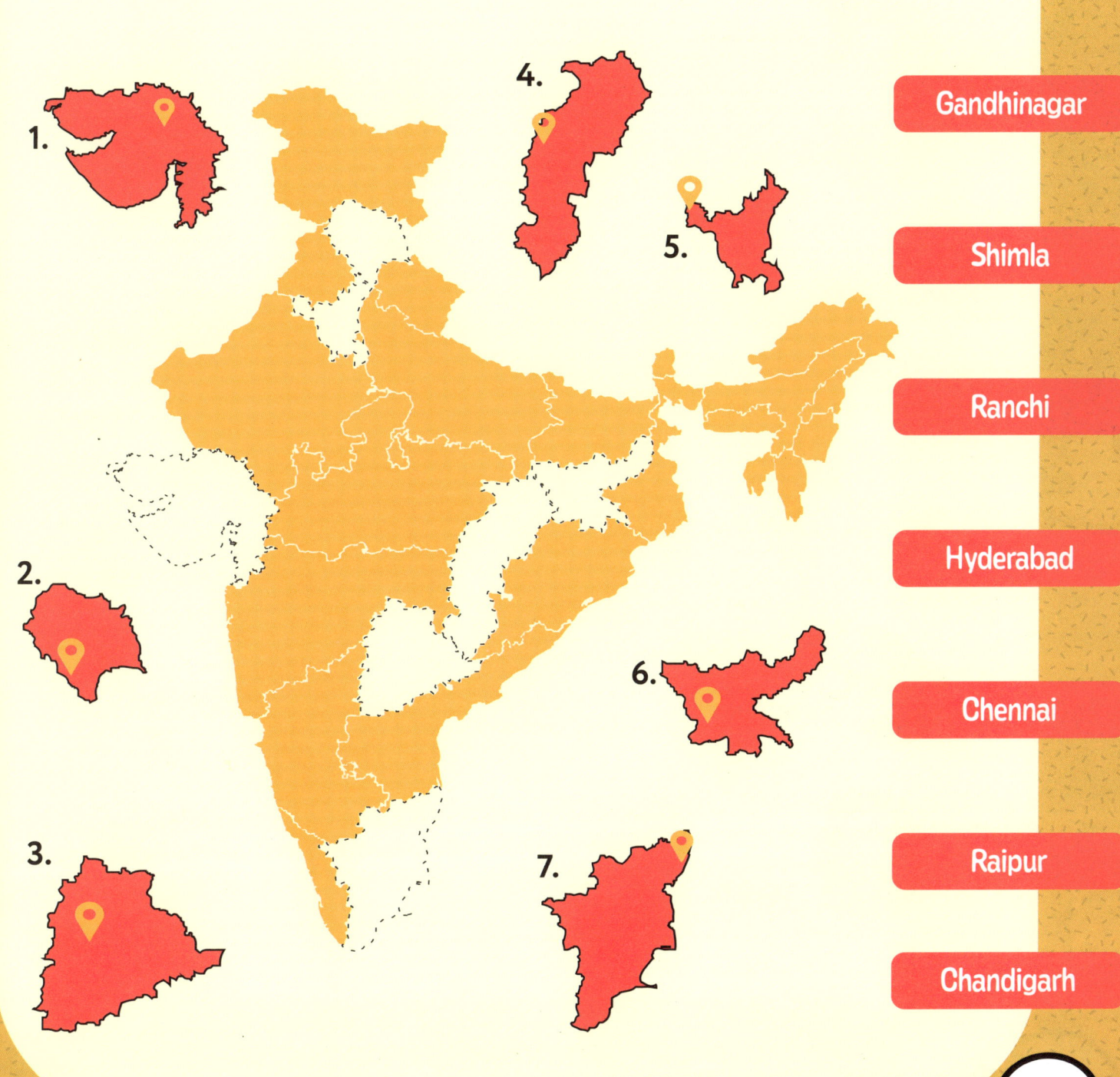

STATE ANIMALS OF INDIA

Draw a line to match each state with its state animal!

 ASIATIC LION

 ONE-HORNED RHINOCEROS

 ELEPHANT

 MUSK DEER

 RED PANDA

 SQUIRREL

 SIKKIM

 KARNATAKA

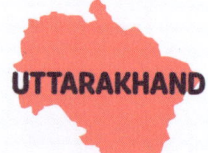 UTTARAKHAND

 MAHARASHTRA

 ASSAM

 GUJARAT

DID YOU KNOW? India is one of the most biodiverse countries in the world, with each state having its own unique state animal to represent its wildlife heritage!

WHOSE SHADOW IS IT?

Look closely at the birds and flowers, then match each to its correct shadow. Can you also name the birds, flowers and the states they belong to?

KNOW YOUR STATES

Fill in the missing words about Indian states!

1. _____ is known as the Land of Tigers.
   A. Rajasthan   B. Assam   C. Madhya Pradesh

2. The famous festival _____ is celebrated in Assam with dance and music.
   A. Baisakhi   B. Onam   C. Bihu

3. The city of _____ is the capital of Kerala and is known for its beautiful backwaters.
   A. Thiruvananthapuram   B. Kochi   C. Chennai

4. The _____ River is the longest river in India.
   A. Ganga   B. Yamuna   C. Godavari

5. _____ is known for its beautiful beaches and Portuguese influence.
   A. Goa   B. Maharashtra   C. Tamil Nadu

6. The famous _____ is an ancient temple in Tamil Nadu, known for its stunning architecture.
   A. Meenakshi Temple   B. Somnath Temple
   C. Golden Temple

MONUMENTS AND HISTORY

Delhi's famous monuments need your help! Follow the dotted lines to complete them. But watch out, some parts like the Qutub Minar's top or the Red Fort's towers are missing. Use your creativity to bring these masterpieces to life!

5

UNRAVEL ROYAL HISTORY!

Travel back in time and become a royal detective! Use the cipher key to crack the code and reveal the name of two famous forts in Rajasthan. Then, write an interesting fact about them in your own words!

ZNYVI ULIG

Cipher Key: Reverse Alphabet Cipher (A = Z, B = Y, C = X.)

Ans: _____

NEMWEPIV JSVX

Each letter has taken 4 steps back (J = N, A = D, I = L.)

Ans: _____

SANGAI FESTIVAL!

Write a short poem about the Sangai deer, Manipur's state animal and illustrate a festival scene featuring this graceful creature.
Use the following words for inspiration:
Graceful, Antlers, Spots, Forest, Majestic, Running free, Endangered, Manipur, Festival, Nature, Wildlife, Beautiful, Peaceful, Celebration

DID YOU KNOW? The Sangai Festival is a celebration of Manipur's rich culture and its unique wildlife, especially the endangered Sangai deer.

TEMPLE HUNT

Find the famous temples of Tamil Nadu! Start at the Kanyakumari Temple and follow the path to Meenakshi Amman Temple, Brihadeshwara, Ramanathaswamy and Shore Temples.

1. Located at the southernmost tip of India, this temple stands where the Arabian Sea, the Bay of Bengal and the Indian Ocean meet—a breathtaking sight at sunset.

5. This 7th-century temple is perched on the shore of the Bay of Bengal and is part of a UNESCO World Heritage Site known for its intricate rock carvings.

HELP THE BAUL SINGER

Help the Baul singer find his way through the intricate paths of Bengal to reach the grand music festival. Along the way, look for hidden treasures of Bengali culture that he can carry to the celebration!

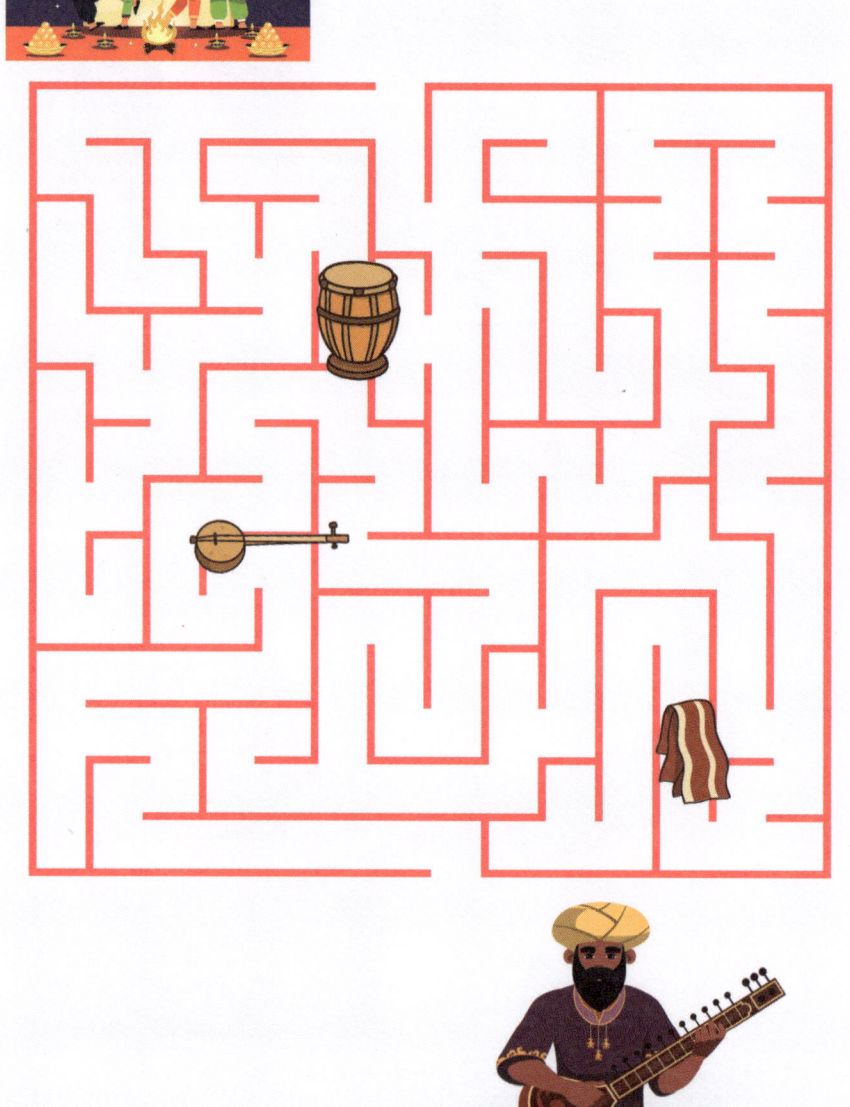

DID YOU KNOW? Baul singers are wandering minstrels from Bengal, known for their soulful songs about love and spirituality.

ROYAL WORDS

Unscramble the jumbled words on this page and uncover some words related to the vibrant colours, rich culture and royal history of Rajasthan.

1.

    RTOF

    _____

2.

    MLEAC

    _____

3.

    EERTSD

    _____

4.

    VEHLAI

    _____

5.

    EPCLAA

    _____

6.

    IAUPJR

    _____

CULTURE CURRY

Find words related to Andhra Pradesh's famous dance forms, food and landmarks!

J	L	A	M	B	A	S	I	N	G	I	A	B	K	W
X	B	I	R	Y	A	N	I	O	Y	R	X	N	D	Z
H	V	N	R	L	R	U	T	T	A	R	A	S	E	P
A	C	U	A	H	E	T	B	K	J	T	Y	S	W	Q
M	Y	P	W	K	D	D	U	W	V	R	N	T	B	R
E	S	I	V	A	H	O	I	T	A	P	U	R	I	T
E	O	P	U	L	I	H	O	R	A	K	H	W	Q	G
S	X	G	R	S	A	N	K	R	A	N	T	I	H	D
A	A	A	E	F	H	G	A	N	D	I	K	O	T	A
L	K	K	N	R	U	S	H	I	K	O	N	D	A	D
A	I	K	R	D	K	O	N	A	S	E	E	M	A	D
Y	L	P	D	I	H	H	B	R	A	M	A	F	S	B
A	I	L	C	P	I	R	I	P	P	Y	K	C	P	A
R	H	H	N	U	M	V	A	R	O	W	Q	M	S	O
N	C	W	K	G	M	K	U	C	H	I	P	U	D	I

WORD BANK

- Rama
- Chilika
- Lambasingi
- Pesarattu
- Sankranti
- Rayalaseema
- Biryani
- Gandikota
- Pulihora
- Araku
- Rushikonda
- Kuchipudi
- Andhra
- Tirupati
- Konaseema

DID YOU KNOW? Kuchipudi is a classical dance form that originated in Andhra Pradesh!

DISCOVER STATE FACTS

Find five hidden words linked to Manipur, Mizoram and Meghalaya in the grid. Match them with their meanings and explore the wonders of these vibrant states!

D	I	A	G	N	A	S	G	I	F
X	B	A	M	B	O	O	R	I	T
U	B	K	O	W	A	U	U	C	L
D	R	C	K	K	A	T	K	O	L
Z	T	O	V	X	D	K	L	U	F
D	O	L	R	E	B	P	X	S	V
V	W	O	V	E	T	H	Z	J	A
V	X	O	T	N	L	I	N	X	Y
A	M	H	Y	W	B	Y	P	K	S
B	G	A	N	D	I	S	A	H	K

1. A rare and endangered brow-antlered deer, found only in Manipur's Loktak Lake region. Known as the 'dancing deer'.

2. An essential plant in the Northeast, especially in states like Mizoram and Tripura, used for construction, food and craft.

3. The largest freshwater lake in Northeast India, located in Manipur, famous for its floating phumdis (islands).

4. An indigenous tribe from Meghalaya, known for their matrilineal society and rich cultural traditions.

5. A type of gibbon (ape) found in the forests of Northeast India, particularly in Arunachal Pradesh and Assam.

DID YOU KNOW? Meghalaya means 'abode of clouds,' and Hoolock Gibbons are one of the many endangered species in the state!

13

DRESS UP FOR BIHU!

Colour the traditional clothes from Assam and add details like accessories and a background to bring the picture to life!

DID YOU KNOW? Bihu is Assam's most famous festival, celebrating the Assamese New Year with traditional dance, music and feasts. It marks the arrival of spring.

ALL MASKED UP!

Kathakali is a traditional dance form from Kerala, known for its expressive masks. Design your own Kathakali mask using colours and patterns that match the character you imagine. Give your mask a unique expression—is it happy, angry or calm?

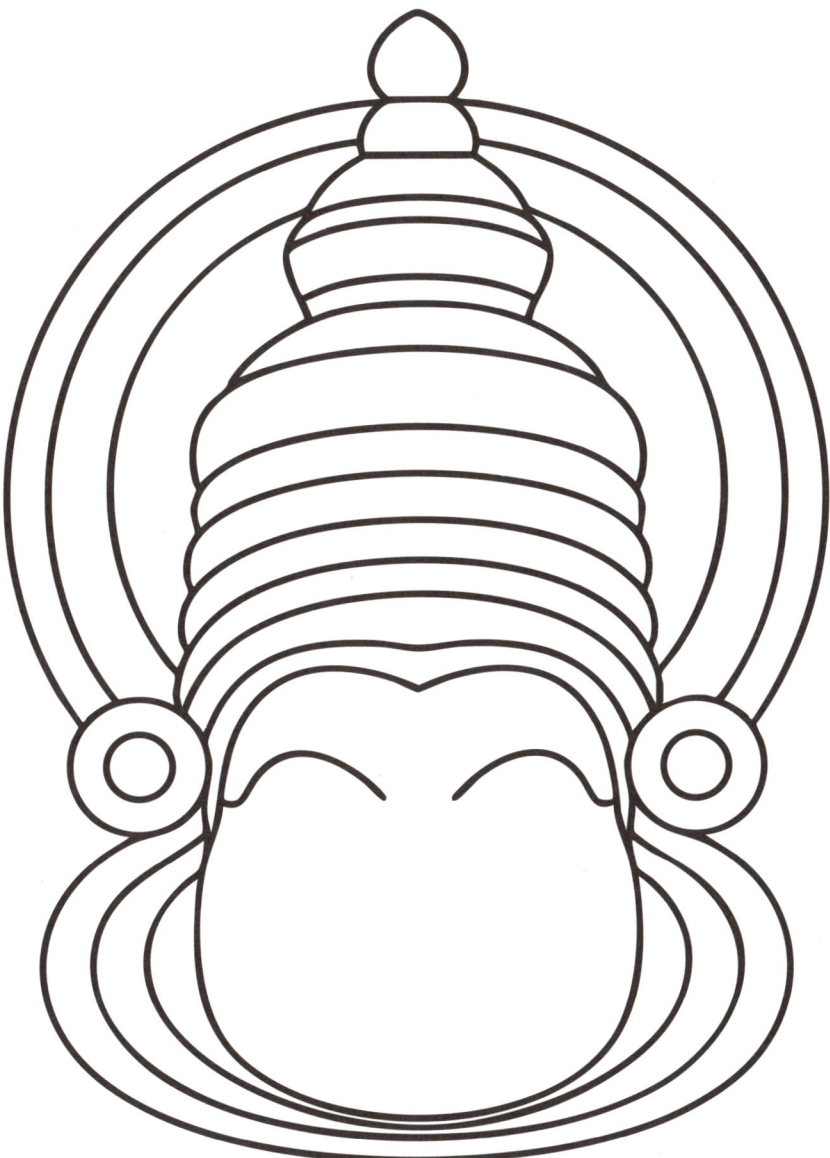

DID YOU KNOW? Kathakali dancers wear big costumes and paint their faces to tell exciting stories from ancient books like the Ramayana and Mahabharata.

15

SEQUENCING ACTIVITY

Dive into the grandeur of Odisha's Rath Yatra! Look at the pictures showing different stages of the festival and arrange them in the correct order to tell the story of this grand celebration.

Bonus Challenge: For each stage, write one sentence describing what is happening in the picture. How much do you know about this vibrant festival?

The arrival of the chariots at Gundicha Temple.

A

Priests dressing the idols of Lord Jagannath, Balabhadra and Subhadra.

B

Return journey of the chariots, called the Bahuda Yatra.

C

The deities being carried out in a ceremonial procession to the chariots (Pahandi Bije).

D

Carpenters carving and decorating the wooden chariots.

E

The chariots travelling through bustling crowd, with people showering flowers.

F

The massive chariots being pulled by devotees.

G

16

Stage 1 :

Stage 2 :

Stage 3 :

Stage 4 :

Stage 5 :

Stage 6 :

Stage 7 :

DID YOU KNOW? Odisha's Rath Yatra in Puri is one of the largest and oldest chariot festivals in the world, where huge chariots carrying the deities are pulled by thousands of devotees in a grand procession!

TREASURES OF GUJARAT

Can you find these hidden items in the picture?

KITE   CHARKHA

POT   DANDIYA STICKS

DID YOU KNOW? Gujarat is famous for its kite festival, Uttarayan, where people fly colourful kites in the sky, creating a vibrant spectacle!

18

GUESS THE POPULATION!

Look at the images below. Each circle stands for people; more circles in an image means the state has more people.
Now, answer the questions given below and match each image to the correct state.

SIKKIM — A

B — **MAHARASHTRA**

TAMIL NADU — C

D — **UTTAR PRADESH**

1. Which state has the highest population, in India?
2. Which state has the lowest population, in India?
3. Which images represent the remaining states?

Hint: Maharashtra is more populated than Tamil Nadu.

DID YOU KNOW ? India is the most populous country in the world! That's more than 1.4 billion people!

19

THE GREAT GRAIN GAME

Chhattisgarh is often called the Rice Bowl of India because it grows so many varieties of rice. Unscramble these words related to rice and Chhattisgarh and then match each word to the correct fact!

CIER
....

ADPDY
....

RIDP RIRIAGONTI
....

HASTICHARGH
....

KHAPLA
....

MATCH THE WORDS TO THE FACTS

- The grain harvested from rice plants before the husk is removed
- A white grain staple of Chhattisgarh
- A famous rice dish from Chhattisgarh made with curd and spices
- A farming method used to grow rice with minimal water
- The state where these delicious rice traditions come from!

DID YOU KNOW? The Chitrakote Waterfall in Chhattisgarh is the widest in India. It is often compared to Niagara Falls, especially during the monsoon.

CHHATH PUJA MATH

Ready for a festive fraction challenge? At the Chhath Puja festival this year, 120 people took a holy dip at the village pond. If three-fourths of the people offered fruits and one-fourth offered flowers to the Sun God. Can you calculate the number of people who offered flowers?

Ans: _____

BACKWATERS

Meera says Kerala's backwaters are one of the state's greatest attractions. But she doesn't know their total length.

Here's what she claims to know:
- Lake V is 230 kilometres long
- Canal P is 40 kilometres long
- All other canals together are 80 kilometres long.

Can you help Meera figure out the total length of Kerala's backwaters?

_____

THE BEACH COUNT

Unscramble the words to discover names of a few Goa's beaches and match them to their fun facts!

GABA

MRARIMA

AAGORTV

UANJAN

LOVCA

1. Nestled near red cliffs, this beach is quieter but loved for its dramatic sunsets and great views of Chapora Fort.

2. One of the most happening beaches, packed with nightlife and water sports.

3. A golden stretch of sand close to Panaji, perfect for evening strolls and calm waves, popular with locals and tourists alike.

4. A long, wide beach in South Goa known for its white sand, swaying palms and peaceful charm.

5. Known for its flea markets and hippie past.

JUICY APPLES!

Apples from Himachal Pradesh come in all colours. Can you spot them all in the picture? Look carefully and find:
- Red apples
- Green apples
- Yellow apples

How many apples are there? Also find a basket of apples.

DID YOU KNOW? Himachal Pradesh is known for its apple orchards, especially in areas like Kullu and Shimla!

ASSAM'S TEA PLANTATION MAZE

Guide the tea picker through the maze to the tea garden in Assam!

DID YOU KNOW? Assam is one of the largest tea-producing regions in the world!

WILDLIFE WATCH

Step into the jungle of Uttarakhand and explore the Jim Corbett National Park! Match the footprints to their animals, then draw your favourite creature from the park. Imagine spotting a tiger, an elephant or a crocodile in the wild!

 1.    2.    3.    4.

Draw your favourite animal from Jim Corbett!

DID YOU KNOW? Jim Corbett National Park was India's first national park and is famous for its Bengal tigers!

GUESS THE STATE

Solve the riddles to name the states of India!

1. I'm the land of rivers, tea gardens and the famous Kaziranga, where rhinos roam. _____

2. I'm the home of the mighty Himalayas and my capital is the city of 'Shimla'. _____

3. I'm the state of golden sands, forts and camels and my capital is Jaipur. _____

4. I'm the state known for its backwaters, beaches and the serene houseboats. _____

5. I'm famous for the Taj Mahal and my capital city is Agra. _____

6. I'm the state with a rich history of kings and palaces and my capital is Bhopal. _____

7. I'm the state of tea gardens, the famed Darjeeling and the Kanchenjunga peak. _____

8. I'm the coastal state with beautiful beaches, seafood and vibrant festivals. _____

9. I'm known for my tea estates, orchids and Sikkimese culture. _____

10. I'm the state with famous temples, silk weaving and the city of Mysuru. _____

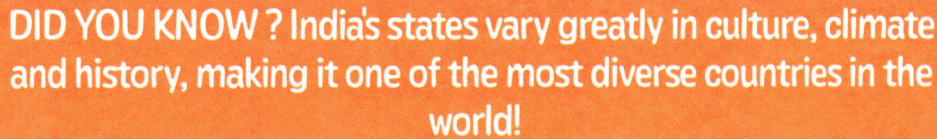

DID YOU KNOW ? India's states vary greatly in culture, climate and history, making it one of the most diverse countries in the world!

MAGIC BUILDING TIME

Let's make Charminar pretty!

DID YOU KNOW? Charminar in Hyderabad is one of India's most iconic monuments! It's known for its four grand arches and towers and is a symbol of the city's rich history and culture.

FIND THE WORDS

Hidden in the grid are some words associated with the Northeastern state of Nagaland. Circle the words with a pencil or pen!

X	Z	Z	B	B	S	H	B	A	A
O	O	B	M	A	B	O	G	Y	C
O	L	N	A	G	A	R	C	O	F
A	Q	W	S	E	A	N	C	Q	E
E	J	Y	C	Q	D	B	V	H	S
Y	D	N	E	Y	G	I	Q	E	T
K	A	J	D	T	H	L	G	B	I
D	O	W	Q	P	M	L	J	I	V
P	Y	J	L	R	I	C	E	R	A
X	V	T	G	F	G	V	J	T	L

Naga   Hornbill   Rice

Bamboo   Festival

DID YOU KNOW? Nagaland is home to many different tribes, each with their own language and customs!

29

THE RIVERS OF INDIA

Get ready to explore the lifelines of this country! On this map of India, you'll find rivers like the Ganga, Godavari, Brahmaputra, Krishna and Narmada flowing through the land. Your task is to identify the states each river flows through and mark them.

DID YOU KNOW ? The Ganga is the longest river in India and holds immense cultural and spiritual significance for millions of people!

SIKKIM'S SNOW LEOPARD SEARCH

Look closely at these two pictures of Sikkim's snowy mountains. Can you spot the hiding snow leopards?

DID YOU KNOW? Sikkim is home to the elusive snow leopard, a rare and majestic animal that thrives in high altitudes and snowy terrains!

LITERARY LEGENDS

Match these celebrated Bengali authors to their famous works!

RABINDRANATH TAGORE

A. PATHER PANCHALI

BANKIM CHANDRA CHATTOPADHYAY

B. ANANDAMATH

BIBHUTIBHUSHAN BANDYOPADHYAY

C. GITANJALI

SARAT CHANDRA CHATTOPADHYAY

D. DEVDAS

SUNIL GANGOPADHYAY

E. SEI SAMAY

DID YOU KNOW? Rabindranath Tagore was the first non-European to win the Nobel Prize in Literature in 1913!

THE RAJPUT RIDDLE

Long ago, in a royal kingdom, a Rajput king had 100 horses. He decided to gift some to his sons:

He gave ¼ of them to his eldest son.

He gave ⅓ of them to his youngest son.

- Use your math skills to solve this royal riddle! Figure out how many horses did the king leave behind.
- Circle the correct answer from the options below:

A) 50 B) 60

C) 70 D) 75

DID YOU KNOW? Rajasthan is known for its rich history, royal heritage, and majestic forts. The Rajput kings built beautiful forts like Amber Fort and Mehrangarh Fort, which stand as symbols of their strength and pride!

COFFEE PLANTATION CHALLENGE

Get ready for a fun coffee adventure! Search for the hidden words in the puzzle related to Karnataka's amazing coffee plantations. Words can go up, down, or even diagonally! Can you find them all? Once you're done, imagine sipping a yummy hot chocolate in the cool coffee hills of Karnataka!

P	L	A	N	T	A	T	I	O	N
F	A	A	L	E	E	F	F	O	C
O	C	V	O	O	X	Z	E	W	L
R	I	A	S	E	S	D	N	C	D
O	B	J	A	E	I	L	G	U	J
B	A	G	A	A	T	R	L	U	Y
U	R	U	P	J	O	A	S	I	V
S	A	A	D	O	X	E	T	U	H
T	F	V	C	L	X	H	N	S	W
A	J	B	O	R	E	T	A	G	E

WORD BANK

Arabica	Coorg	Hills
Robusta	Coffee	Java
Plantation	Estates	

DID YOU KNOW? Karnataka is the largest producer of coffee in India!

34

THE JOURNEY OF THE MAHATMA

Put these scenes in the correct order to complete Gandhi's journey!

Gandhi leaves Gujarat for England

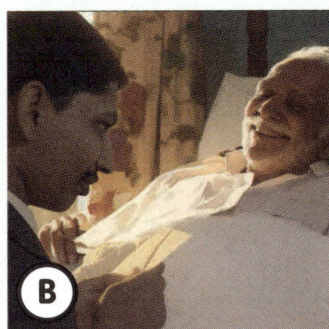
Gandhi admitting his mistake to his father

Gandhi as a child refusing to eat meat

Young Gandhi learning discipline at school in Rajkot

Gandhi visiting a temple despite caste restrictions

Gandhi reading books about truth and non-violence

1. .... 2. .... 3. ....

4. .... 5. .... 6. ....

DID YOU KNOW? Sabarmati Ashram in Gujarat was one of Mahatma Gandhi's primary residences and is now a museum dedicated to his life and legacy.

FESTIVALS OF INDIA

Use the clues to match the festivals with the correct states. Test your knowledge of India's diverse culture and traditions!

States	Diwali	Onam	Durga puja	Navarati	Pongal
Kerala					
Tamil Nadu					
West Bengal					
Uttar Pradesh					
Gujarat					

1. Diwali is widely celebrated in this state but is not the main festival in Tamil Nadu. _____

2. Onam is the biggest festival in this state and is known for boat races and flower carpets. _____

3. Durga Puja is widely celebrated in this state, especially in Kolkata. _____

4. This state celebrates Pongal, a harvest festival where people cook rice and thank the sun god. _____

5. Navratri is celebrated in this state with colourful Garba dances and night-long celebrations. _____

DID YOU KNOW? Each state in India has unique festivals that showcase its culture and traditions, from the colourful dances of Gujarat to the tranquil boat races of Kerala!

MAHARASHTRA'S MYSTERIES

**Spot fake facts about Maharashtra!
Tell whether they are True or False.**

1. Maharashtra is home to the iconic Gateway of India. ....

2. Mumbai, the capital of Maharashtra, is the capital city of India. ....

3. Maharashtra is known for its famous dance form, Bharatnatyam. ....

4. The famous Ajanta and Ellora Caves are located in Maharashtra. ....

5. Maharashtra's official language is Hindi. ....

6. Maharashtra has the largest number of national parks in India. ....

7. Mumbai is known as the City of Dreams because of its thriving film industry, Bollywood. ....

8. Maharashtra is the birthplace of the great leader, Mahatma Gandhi. ....

9. Maharashtra's state animal is the Bengal Tiger. ....

10. The popular street food in Maharashtra is Vada Pav. ....

DID YOU KNOW? Nagpur is referred to as the winter capital of Maharashtra because the state legislature holds its winter session there.

COUNTING STEPS

Help the mountaineer reach the top by solving these math problems! Each correct answer will take you one step closer to the summit!

DID YOU KNOW? Uttarakhand is home to Nanda Devi, the second-highest mountain in India and the third-highest in the world! It's part of the UNESCO World Heritage Sites

AGRICULTURAL PRODUCE

Spot the odd one out in the list of Haryana's agricultural produce!

I'm a fruit that doesn't grow in Haryana's fields. The others are staple crops that are widely grown in the state

I'm a root vegetable, while the others are tropical fruits grown in Haryana's climate.

I'm a vegetable that's often grown in cooler climates, while the others are more commonly found in Haryana's fields

DID YOU KNOW? Haryana is a major producer of wheat, rice and milk in India!

BIRYANI ADVENTURE

How about making a delicious Hyderabadi biryani? Unscramble the words and fill in the blanks to get the complete recipe.

Step 1: Wash and soak R____E (CERI) in water for 30 minutes.

Step 2: Slice some N_____S (SNOOIN) and fry them until golden brown.

Step 3: Marinate the C_____E (CHEKCIN) with __O_____T (GYOHRUT), ginger-garlic paste, spices and lemon juice. Let it rest for at least an hour.

Step 4: Boil water with whole S_____S (SPEISC) like cardamom, cloves and cinnamon. Parboil the rice until it's half-cooked.

Step 5: In a pot, layer the marinated chicken at the bottom and the R____E (CERI) on top. Add a few strands of __A_____N (FRASFNO) soaked in milk for colour and aroma.

Step 6: Cover the pot tightly and cook on low heat (known as dum cooking) to let the flavours blend the _____ (MEATS) seals in the taste!

Step 7: Garnish with fried onions, fresh mint and coriander before serving.

DID YOU KNOW? Hyderabadi biryani is known for its unique dum cooking technique, where the dish is slow-cooked with a sealed lid to trap the steam and flavours

FIND THE HIDDEN DANCE FORMS

Find all the famous dance forms of Odisha hidden in this puzzle! Words can be horizontal, vertical, or diagonal.

I	Y	U	M	V	H	W	L	Z	M
R	A	A	H	T	B	Q	S	P	M
U	U	H	S	X	F	D	Y	H	Z
P	P	H	W	J	H	L	Q	G	Y
L	I	C	N	K	X	V	H	C	M
A	T	I	S	S	I	D	O	A	N
B	O	P	B	R	O	V	H	Z	V
M	G	C	T	L	B	A	O	J	R
A	B	X	S	Y	R	Z	F	C	I
S	O	V	E	I	H	I	S	H	A

Word Bank

Odissi Gotipua

Mahari Chhau

Sambalpuri

DID YOU KNOW? Odissi, known for its grace and fluidity was performed in temples to honour deities!

NATURAL WONDERS

Can you solve the clues and complete the word pyramid? Each word is linked to Meghalaya's stunning landscapes and unique attractions. Use the hints below to climb to the top of the pyramid!

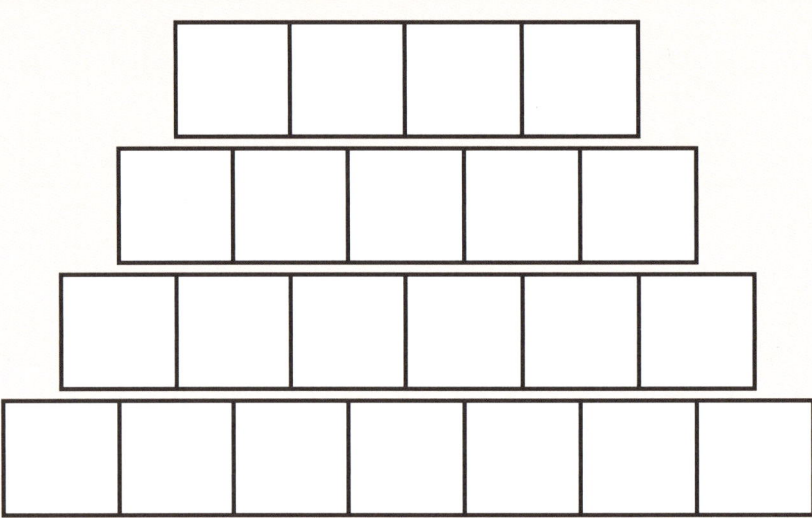

Level 1 (4 letters) :

Hint: Commonly found in the caves of Meghalaya, these flying mammals helps pollinate plants and control insects.

Level 2 (5 letters):

Hint: These dark and mysterious places are found under the ground, like Mawsmai.

Level 3 (6 letters):

Hint: Meghalaya's name means the 'Abode of ____.' This is what covers its hills.

Level 4 (7 letters):

Hint: Meghalaya has sacred ones, full of trees and wildlife.

DID YOU KNOW? Meghalaya is home to the famous living root bridges, which are made by growing the roots of trees in a way that forms bridges over streams!

HISTORICAL SITES

Unscramble these words to uncover Uttar Pradesh's rich history and iconic landmarks! Each word represents a historical site or a cultural gem.

- AJT AHMLA
- FARUTEPH RISIK
- ASNAAVRI
- GARA OTFR
- APPART RAGH
- ABAR IMMABAAR
- AANGG AHGT

DID YOU KNOW? Uttar Pradesh is the only state in India that houses three UNESCO World Heritage Sites: the Taj Mahal, Agra Fort and Fatehpur Sikri!

HOMES OF MIZORAM

Design a traditional bamboo hut like the ones in Mizoram's villages!

DID YOU KNOW? Mizoram is called the 'Land of Bamboo' as bamboo forests cover most of the state

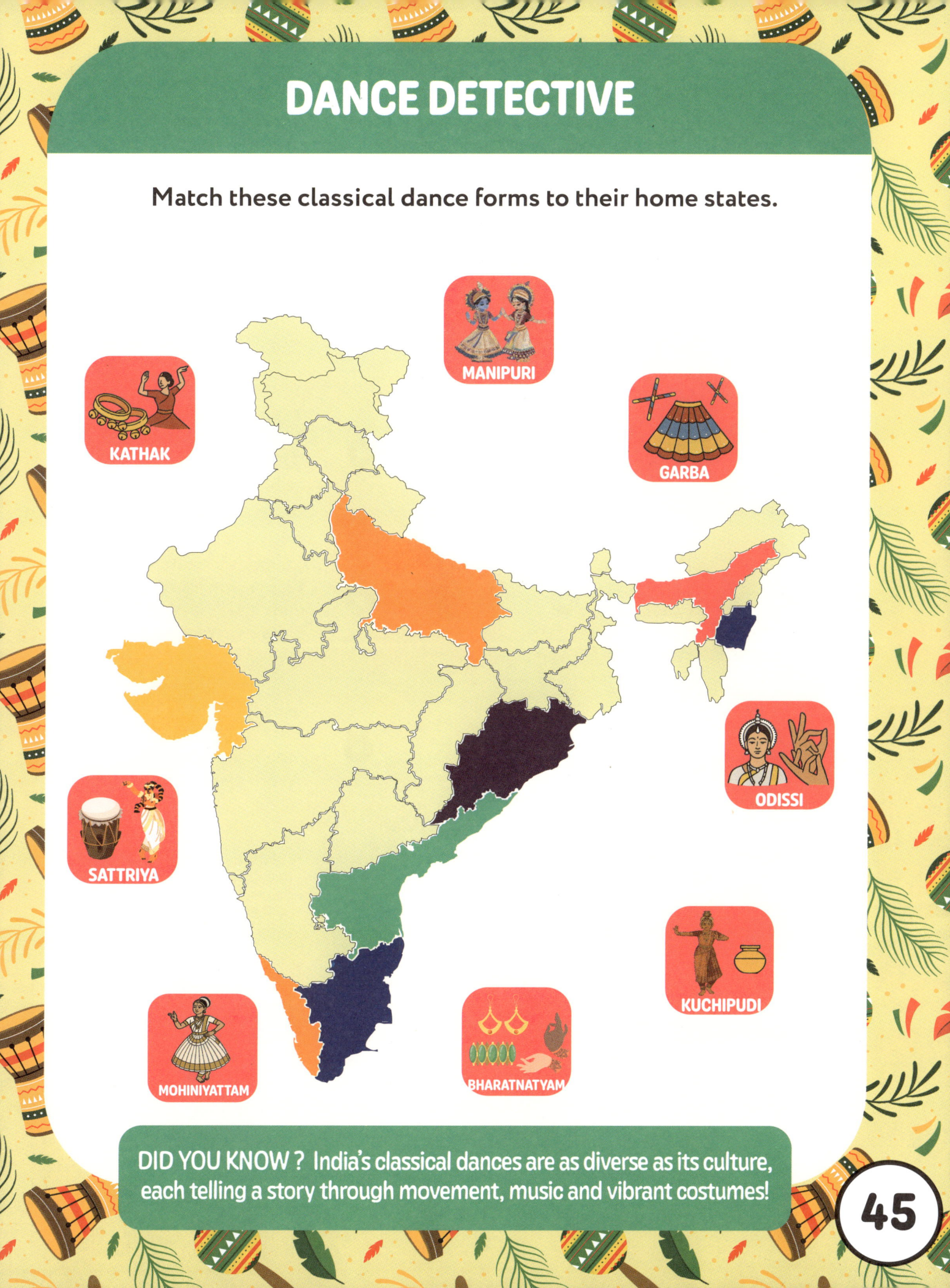

FAMOUS BRIDGES OF THE WORLD

Let's match these famous bridges with their descriptions.

 ○   ○ The iconic bridge in Kolkata, India, known for its massive steel structure.

 ○   ○ Famous suspension bridge in San Francisco, USA, known for its vibrant red colour.

 ○   ○ A famous bascule and suspension bridge in London, UK, known for its twin towers.

 ○   ○ The cable-stayed bridge in Mumbai, India, connecting Bandra to Worli over the sea.

 ○   ○ A railway bridge in Tamil Nadu, India, connecting the town of Rameswaram to mainland India.

 ○   ○ The longest suspension bridge in the world, connecting the Japanese islands of Honshu and Shikoku

DID YOU KNOW? The Howrah Bridge was built in just six years, without using nuts or bolts.

FLAVOURS OF INDIA

Match the food to the state it comes from!

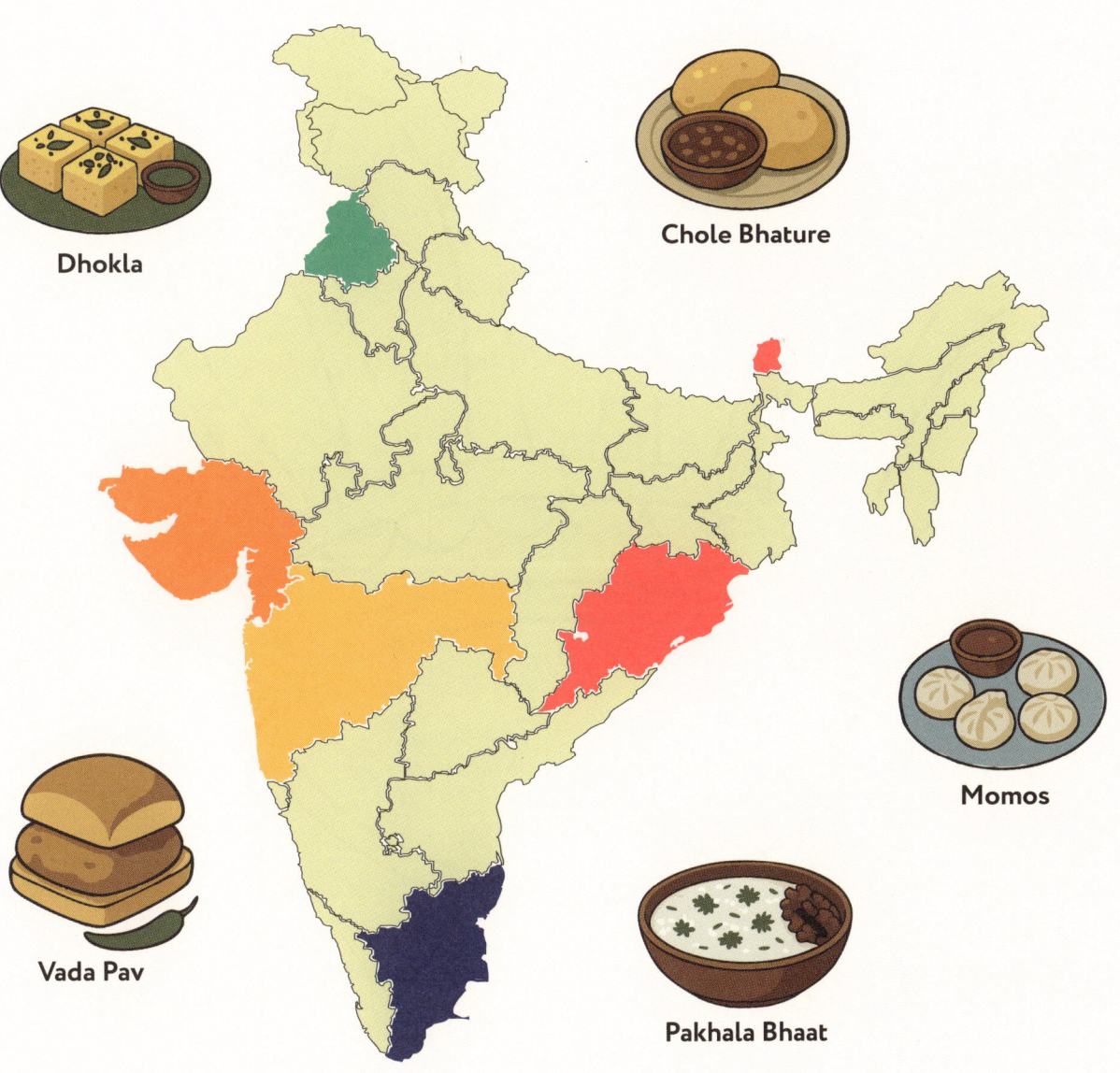

Can you design your own unique dish by combining ingredients from two different states? Draw your food masterpiece!

47

TRIBAL HEADGEAR CRAFTING

Design a traditional tribal headgear from Arunachal Pradesh. Use feathers, beads, and other materials you can think of to decorate it!

DID YOU KNOW? Many indigenous tribes of Arunachal Pradesh wear beautifully crafted headgear made of feathers, beads and other natural materials

NATURAL WONDERS

Complete the sentences to discover Jammu and Kashmir.

1. _____ Lake is a famous destination in Kashmir, known for its houseboats and scenic views.
   A. Dal   B. Nagin   C. Wular

2. _____ Valley is often referred to as the 'Valley of Flowers' due to its vibrant flowers in bloom.
   A. Kulu   B. Gulmarg   C. Poonch

3. _____ is the largest freshwater lake in Jammu & Kashmir and a popular spot for boating and bird-watching.
   A. Wular   B. Nagin   C. Dal

4. The famous _____ Garden in Srinagar is known for its Mughal architecture and terraced gardens.
   A. Nishat   B. Shalimar   C. Tulip

5. _____ Peak is one of the highest points in Jammu & Kashmir, popular for trekking and mountaineering.
   A. Vaishno Devi   B. Mount Harmukh   C. Amarnath

DID YOU KNOW? Kashmir is known as 'Paradise on Earth' for its stunning landscapes and natural beauty!

UNSCRAMBLE THE STATE NAMES

Can you unscramble these jumbled state names? Each word is mixed up, but once you solve it, you'll know which state it belongs to! What's the official language of each state?

Scrambled State Name	Hints	Language
SAMAS	Famous for tea gardens and silk!	
SHADIO	Home to the sun temple!	
JANARSTHA	Where the Great Indian Desert is!	
RANAHYA	Known for its capital, Chandigarh!	
LAEKAR	The home of Kathakali dance!	
HARMASTRAHA	Has the famous Ajanta caves!	
GAYELHAMA	It's capital is known as the 'Scotland of East'!	
KANKAATAR	This state is famous for sandalwood!	
KARUTADHANT	Known for the river Ganga!	
DAPESHYAMRAD	Land of the White Tiger Reserve!	

50

LANDMARK MATCHING GAME

Match the landmarks to their corresponding cities in Bihar. Can you identify them all?

Patna Sahib Gurudwara

Bodh Gaya

Nalanda ruins

○   ○   ○

MAHABODHI TEMPLE   **NALANDA**   **PATNA**

DID YOU KNOW? Bihar is the seat of the first university in the world--Nalanda University! Students from many countries came there to learn and live!

KERALA TO JAMMU AND KASHMIR ADVENTURE

Starting from Kerala, take an adventurous journey to reach Jammu and Kashmir. Trace two paths—one through the maximum number of states and one through the least. Draw up your list and ask a friend to draw up theirs and compare.

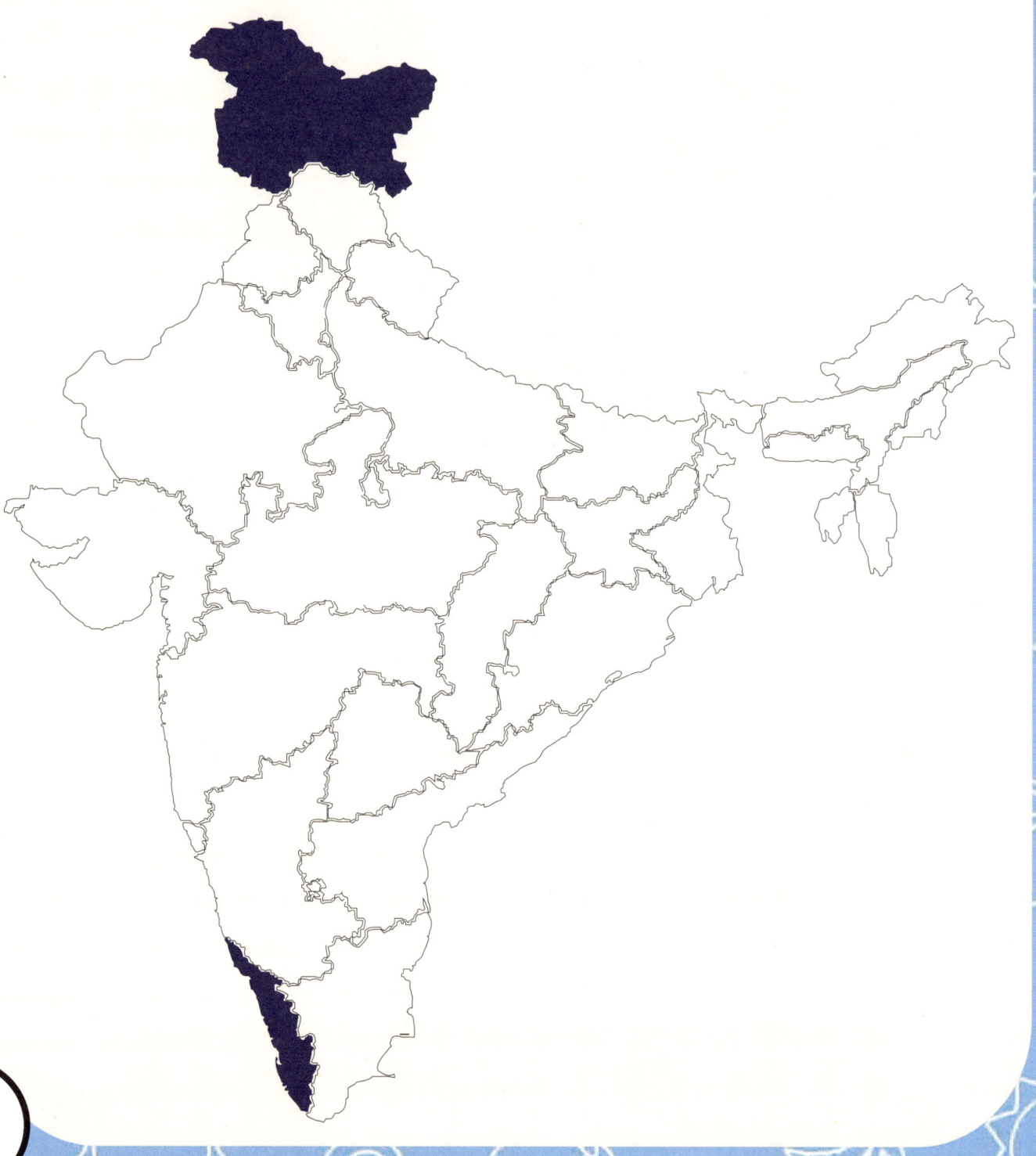

IDENTIFY CROPS OF INDIA

Can you match each crop to the state it's best known for?
See if you can pair them correctly!

| Rice | Tea | Cotton | Sugar Cane | Spices |

○ ○ ○ ○ ○

○ ○ ○ ○ ○

Gujarat Kerala Assam West Bengal Uttar Pradesh

DID YOU KNOW? India is one of the largest producers of agricultural crops and each state has its own specialty!

CREATE FOLK ART

Colour the folk art styles, match them to their states and design your own folk art!

Warli

Bright temple art with red, green and gold

Madhubani

Intricate pen-drawn designs

Kalamkari

Vibrant depictions of nature and gods

Kerala Mural Art

Made of circles, triangles and lines

Design Your Own Folk Art

MAKE THE MAP!

Connect the dots to make Madhya Pradesh! Also identify the notable landmarks and which cities they are located in

○　　　　　　　○　　　　　　　○

KHAJURAHO TEMPLE　　**SANCHI STUPA**　　**GWALIOR FORT**

DID YOU KNOW? Madhya Pradesh is home to the ancient Kanha National Park, which inspired Rudyard Kipling's *The Jungle Book* and is known for its amazing wildlife, including tigers and leopards!

INDIA'S NATIONAL PARKS CHALLENGE

Complete the activity and match the animals with their national parks in India!

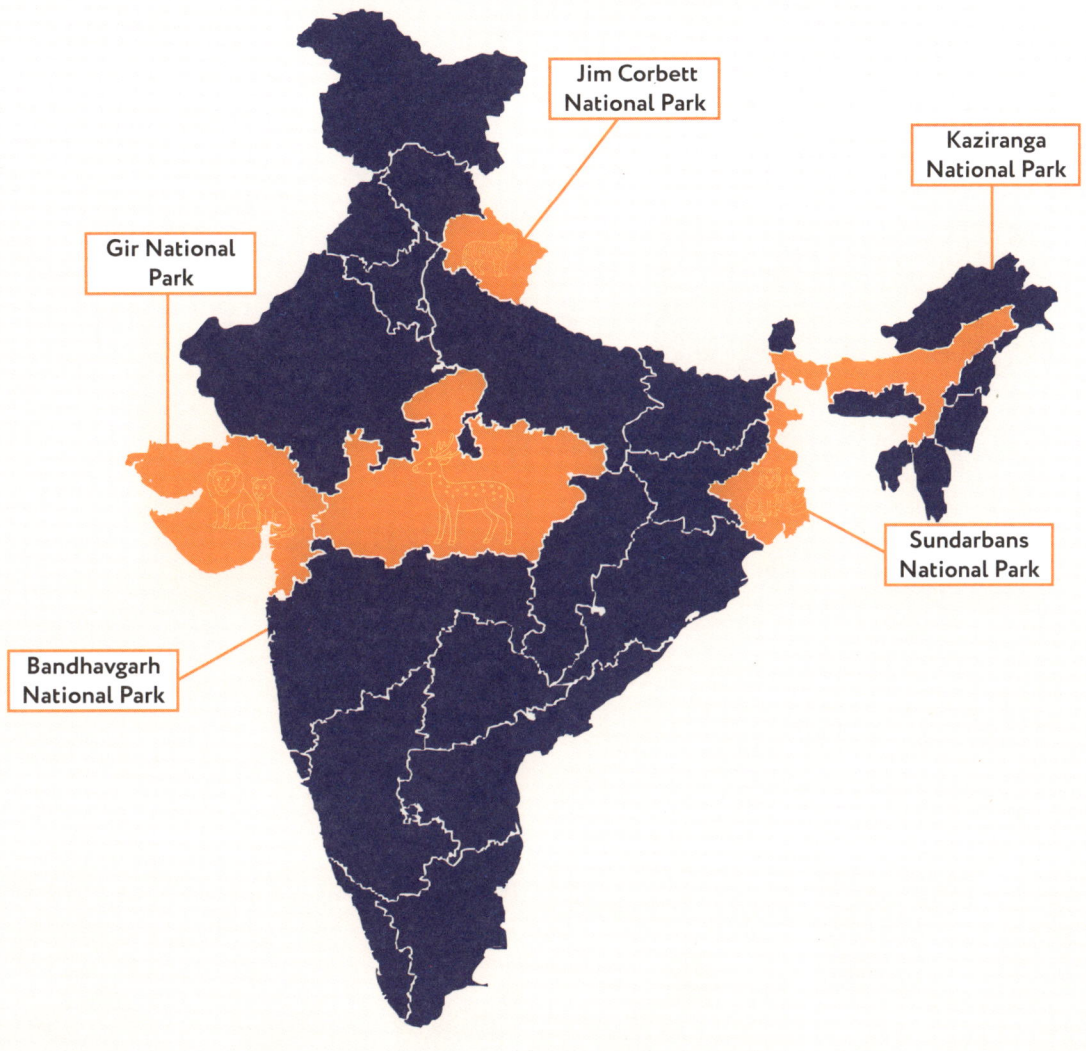

1. Famous for one-horned _____ (*Hint: A large, endangered animal with a single horn*)

2. Known for _____ (*Hint: India's national animal, a big cat*)

3. Home to _____ (*Hint: A wild cat known for its swimming ability*)

4. Famous for its large tiger population and _____ (*Hint: A large herbivorous mammal, found in forests*)

5. The only home of _____ lions in the world (*Hint: A species of lion found only in this park*)

57

Count the Wonders

Can you count all the hidden objects in these scenes from Tripura?

Count the fish in the lake. How many fish in total?

How many trees in total?

....

Count the monkeys, birds, and deer in the sanctuary scene.

How many horses are walking?

Count the number of windows in the Ujjayanta Palace.

....

DID YOU KNOW? The Ganga is the longest river in India and holds immense cultural and spiritual significance for millions of people!

ANSWERS

Page 1:
1. Gujarat-Gandhinagar
2. Himachal-Shimla
3. Telengana-Hyderabad
4. Chhatisgarh-Ranchi
5. Haryana-Chandigarh
6. Jharkhand-Ranchi
7. Tamil Nadu-Raipur

Page 2 :
Asiatic Lion → Gujarat
One-Horned Rhinoceros → Assam
Elephant → Karnataka
Musk Deer → Uttarakhand
Red Panda → Sikkim
Squirrel → Maharashtra

Page 3:
1-D; Kerala-Great Hornbill-Golden Shower
2-A; Gujarat-Greater Flamingo-Marigold
3-B; Punjab-Northern Shrike-Lotus
4-C; Tamil Nadu-Asian Koel-Gloriosa Lily

Page 4 :
1. Madhya Pradesh
2. Bihu
3. Thiruvananthapuram
4. Ganga
5. Goa
6. Meenakshi Temple

Page 6 :
1. AMBER FORT
2. JAISALMER FORT

Page 8-9 :
A. Kanyakumari Temple (Kanyakumari)
B. Meenakshi Amman Temple (Madurai)
C. Brihadeshwara Temple (Thanjavur)
D. Ramanathaswamy Temple (Rameswaram)
E. Shore Temple (Mahabalipuram)

Page 10 :

Page 11 :
1. FORT
2. CAMEL
3. DESERT
4. HAVELI
5. PALACE
6. RAJPUT.

Page 12 :

[word search grid with: LAMBASINGI, BIRYANI, UTTARA, SIVAHO, ITAPURI, PULIHORA, SANKRANTI, GANDIKOTA, RUSHIKONDA, KONASEEMA, BRAMA, KUCHIPUDI]

Page 13 :

[word search grid with: AGNAS, BAMBOO, KATKOL, ISAH, GAND, H column]

1-Sangai
2-Bamboo
3-Loktak
4- Khasi
5-Hoolock

Page 16 & 17 :
1 e, 2 b, 3 d, 4 g, 5 f, 6 a, 7 c

Page 18 :

Page 19 :
1. Highest population-Uttar Pradesh
2. Lowest population-Sikkim
A-Uttar Pradeh
B-Sikkim
C-Tamil Nadu
D-Maharashtra

Page 20 :
CIER → RICE
ADPDY → PADDY
RIDP RIRIAGONTI – DRIP IRRIGATION
HASTICHARGH → CHHATTISGARH
KHAPLA → PAKHAL

Page 21 :
30 people offered flowers to the Sun God.

Page 22 :
230+40+80=350 kilometres

Page 23 :
1-VAGATOR
2-BAGA
3-MIRAMAR
4-COLVA
5-ANJUNA

ANSWERS

Page 24 :

Red apples - 7
Yellow apples - 13
Green apples - 14

Page 25 :

Page 26:
1-Crocodile
2-Deer
3-Tiger
4-Elephant

Page 27 :
1. Assam
2. Himachal Pradesh
3. Rajasthan
4. Kerala
5. Uttar Pradesh
6. Madhya Pradesh
7. West Bengal
8. Goa
9. Sikkim
10. Karnataka

Page 29 :

X	Z	Z	B	B	S	H	B	A	A
O	O	B	M	A	B	O	G	Y	C
O	L	N	A	G	A	R	C	O	F
A	Q	W	S	E	A	N	C	Q	E
E	J	Y	C	Q	D	B	V	H	S
Y	D	N	E	Y	G	I	Q	E	T
K	A	J	D	T	H	L	G	B	I
D	O	W	Q	P	M	L	J	I	V
P	Y	J	L	R	I	C	E	R	A
X	V	T	G	F	G	V	J	T	L

Page 30:
Brahmaputra-Arunachal Pradesh, Assam, Meghalaya, Nagaland, Sikkim and West Bengal
Ganga-Uttarakhand, Uttar Pradesh, Bihar and West Bengal
Narmada-Madhya Pradesh, Gujarat and Maharashtra
Godavari-Maharashtra, Telangana, Andhra Pradesh and Odisha
Krishna-Maharashtra, Karnataka, Andhra Pradesh and Telangana

Page 31 :

Page 32 :

Rabindranath Tagore – Gitanjali

Sarat Chandra Chattopadhyay – Devdas

Bankim Chandra Chattopadhyay – Anandamath

Bibhutibhushan Bandyopadhyay – Pather Panchali

Sunil Gangopadhyay – Sei Samay

Page 33 :

Option A : 50

Page 34 :

P	L	A	N	T	A	T	I	O	N
F	A	A	L	E	E	F	F	O	C
O	C	V	O	O	X	Z	E	W	L
R	I	A	S	E	S	D	N	C	D
O	B	J	A	E	I	L	G	U	J
B	A	G	A	A	T	R	L	U	Y
U	R	U	P	J	O	A	S	I	V
S	A	A	D	O	X	E	T	U	H
T	F	V	C	L	X	H	N	S	W
A	J	B	O	R	E	T	A	G	E

Page 35 :
1.C , 2.B , 3.E , 4.D , 5.F , 6.A

Page 36 :
1. Uttar Pradesh
2. Kerala
3. West Bengal
4. Tamil Nadu
5. Gujarat

Page 37 :
1. True   2. False
3. False   4. True
5. False   6. False
7. True   8. False
9. False   10. True

Page 38 :
5 + 3 = 8
8 - 2 = 6
12 ÷ 3 = 4
15 - 7 = 8
10 + 6 = 16

ANSWERS

Page 39:
1-Apple; 2-Potato; 3-Cauliflower

Page 40:
1. RICE; 2. ONIONS; 3. CHICKEN, YOGHURT; 4. SPICES; 5. RICE, SAFFRON; 6. STEAM

Page 41:

I	Y	U	M	V	H	W	L	Z	M
R	A	A	H	T	B	Q	S	P	M
U	U	H	S	X	F	D	Y	H	Z
P	P	H	W	J	H	L	Q	G	Y
L	I	C	N	K	X	V	H	C	M
A	T	I	S	S	I	D	O	A	N
B	O	P	B	R	O	V	H	Z	V
M	G	C	T	L	B	A	O	J	R
A	B	X	S	Y	R	Z	F	C	I
S	O	V	E	I	H	I	S	H	A

Page 42:
1. BATS 2. CAVES 3. CLOUDS 4. FORESTS

Page 43:
AJT AHMLA – Taj Mahal
FARUTEPH RISIK – Fatehpur Sikri
ASNAAVRI – Varanasi
GARA OTFR – Agra Fort
APPART RAGH – Pratapgarh
ABAR IMMABAAR – Bara Imambara
AANG AHGT – Ganga Ghat

Page 45:
Kathak – Uttar Pradesh; Manipuri – Manipur; Garba – Gujarat; Odissi – Odisha; Kuchipudi – Andhra Pradesh; Bharatanatyam – Tamil Nadu; Mohiniyattam – Kerala; Sattriya – Assam

Page 46:
1. Pamban Bridge (Rameswaram Bridge) - A railway bridge in Tamil Nadu, India, connecting the town of Rameswaram to mainland India.
2. Howrah Bridge - The iconic bridge in Kolkata, India, known for its massive steel structure.
3. Bandra-Worli Sea Link - The cable-stayed bridge in Mumbai, India, connecting Bandra to Worli over the sea.
4. Golden Gate Bridge - Famous suspension bridge in San Francisco, USA, known for its vibrant red colour.
5. Tower Bridge - A famous bascule and suspension bridge in London, UK, known for its twin towers.
6. Akashi Kaikyō Bridge - The longest suspension bridge in the world, connecting the Japanese islands of Honshu and Shikoku.

Page 47:
Dhokla – Gujarat; Chole Bhature – Punjab; Momos – Sikkim; Vada Pav – Maharashtra; Pakhala Bhaat – Odisha

Page 49:
1 A. Dal; 2 B. Gulmarg; 3 A. Wular; 4 B. Shalimar; 5 B. Mount Harmukh

Page 50:
Assam – Assamese; Odisha – Odia; Rajasthan – Hindi; Haryana – Haryanvi/Punjabi; Kerala – Malayalam; Maharashtra – Marathi; Meghalaya – English; Karnataka – Kannada; Uttarakhand – Hindi; Madhya Pradesh – Hindi

Page 51:
Patna Sahib Gurudwara → PATNA
Nalanda ruins → NALANDA
Bodh Gaya (Mahabodhi Temple) → MAHABODHI TEMPLE

Page 53:
Rice → West Bengal
Tea → Assam
Cotton → Gujarat
Sugar Cane → Uttar Pradesh
Spices → Kerala

Page 54 & 55:
Warli: Maharashtra (Made of circles, triangles and lines)
Madhubani: Bihar (Vibrant depictions of nature and gods)
Kalamkari: Andhra Pradesh (Intricate pen-drawn designs)
Kerala Mural Art: Kerala (Bright temple art with red, green, and gold)

Page 56:
(brown temple) → Khajuraho Temple
(green structure) → Sanchi Stupa
(blue fort) → Gwalior Fort

Page 57:
1. Rhinos - Kaziranga National Park, Assam; 2. Tigers - Jim Corbett National Park, Uttarakhand; 3. Royal Bengal Tigers - Sundarbans National Park, West Bengal; 4. Chital - Bandhavgarh National Park, Madhya Pradesh; 5. Asiatic lions - Gir National Park, Gujarat

Page 58:
1. 5 goldfish, 3 catfish, 4 carp
2. There are 4 huts with 2 trees beside each
4. Two monkeys, 1 deer and 2 birds
5. 9

OTHER BOOK IN THE SERIES